HEARTBEATS ON PAPER

CAPTURING THE RHYTHM OF THE HEART AND MIND

DIVIJA BAKLIWAL

Copyright © Divija Bakliwal
All Rights Reserved.

This book has been self-published with all reasonable efforts taken to make the material error-free by the author. No part of this book shall be used, reproduced in any manner whatsoever without written permission from the author, except in the case of brief quotations embodied in critical articles and reviews.

The Author of this book is solely responsible and liable for its content including but not limited to the views, representations, descriptions, statements, information, opinions and references ["Content"]. The Content of this book shall not constitute or be construed or deemed to reflect the opinion or expression of the Publisher or Editor. Neither the Publisher nor Editor endorse or approve the Content of this book or guarantee the reliability, accuracy or completeness of the Content published herein and do not make any representations or warranties of any kind, express or implied, including but not limited to the implied warranties of merchantability, fitness for a particular purpose. The Publisher and Editor shall not be liable whatsoever for any errors, omissions, whether such errors or omissions result from negligence, accident, or any other cause or claims for loss or damages of any kind, including without limitation, indirect or consequential loss or damage arising out of use, inability to use, or about the reliability, accuracy or sufficiency of the information contained in this book.

Made with ❤ on the Notion Press Platform
www.notionpress.com

To My Family -

Thank you for being my foundation, my quiet strength, and my constant
source of love.

Contents

Contents

Contents

Foreword

Every book begins with a spark—an idea, a question, a quiet urge to understand the world a little better. This one grew from personal experience, long conversations, and the lessons learned along the way.

It is not just a collection of thoughts, but a reflection of time, growth, and the many people who influenced the journey. Whether you're here to learn, to reflect, or simply to explore, I hope these pages speak to something within you.

Thank you for beginning this journey with me.

Preface

This book was never meant to be a book. It began as scattered thoughts, scribbled verses, and unspoken emotions that needed a place to rest. Over time, they formed a quiet archive of what it means to feel deeply, to hurt quietly, and to heal slowly.

Each poem in these pages is a reflection of something lived—a memory, a moment, or a wound. They speak of invisible struggles, silent battles, and the kind of growth that happens in the dark, when no one is watching. Some were written in pain, some in peace, and many in the uncertain space in between.

I didn't write these poems to impress, but to express. To find clarity in chaos. To remind myself, and perhaps you, that even the softest voice has value. That silence can speak volumes. That healing is not loud—it is patient, messy, and deeply personal.

Thank you for turning these pages and meeting me here.

Welcome to the echoes of my heart.

Acknowledgements

This book would not exist without the quiet strength and unwavering support of the people who stood by me when words failed and emotions overwhelmed.

To my parents—thank you for being my anchor and my light. Your love, understanding, and encouragement gave me the space to explore my voice and heal through it.

To my family and friends who listened patiently, believed in me — I am endlessly grateful.

To every soul who inspired a verse, knowingly or unknowingly—thank you for leaving your mark on these pages.

And to the readers—thank you for holding my words with care. May you find a reflection of yourself in these poems, and may they bring you comfort, clarity, or simply a moment of stillness.

With all my heart, thank you.

Prologue

This collection of poems is a journey through the intricate landscapes of the heart and mind. Each verse is a reflection of the quiet struggles and hidden triumphs we all experience—moments of vulnerability, of joy, of pain, and of healing. These poems are the unspoken words that drift between silences, the stories woven in the spaces between breaths, and the emotions that shape us, yet remain unseen by the world.

They speak to those who feel invisible, to those who fight battles in silence, and to those who seek to find themselves in the midst of life's chaos. These poems are for anyone who has ever felt alone in a crowd, who has lost a part of themselves only to find it again, or who has stood at the crossroads of fate, unsure of which path to take.

This book is not just a collection of words; it is a map of the soul—marking the places we have been, the struggles we have faced, and the peace we seek. In the rhythm of each poem, may you find a connection to the shared experiences that make us human, and in the spaces between the lines, may you discover the comfort of knowing you are never truly alone.

For every heart that beats in silence, for every soul that seeks peace, for every person who has loved, lost, or healed—this book is for you.

1. In your arms, always !

In your arms, I found my start,
A home that beats within my heart.
Your hands have shaped the life I know,
Your love, the soil where I could grow.
Through every storm, you've held me near,
Your steady strength, my shield from fear.
With every smile, with every tear,
Your love has stayed, unshaken, clear.
You are the roots that keep me strong,
The melody within my song.
My parents, my love, my guiding light,
My constant stars in every night.

2. Grandparents: The Roots that Hold Me

Their hands are maps of years gone by,
With stories whispered, soft and sly.
In every hug, a gentle grace,
A lifetime's love in one embrace.
They teach with warmth, not spoken rules,
A quiet strength that time renews.
I'm blessed—they are my living jewels.

3. Mom: My Home Forever

• 3 •

"Mother" is such a simple word;
But to me there's meaning seldom heard;
Watching you, taught me;
What caring and love absolutely are,
And learnt forgiving faults,
Without you, there would be an empty space;
I could never fill, no matter how much i try.
Every memory of time with you;
Is one I'll always treasure.

4. Where The Stars Align

• 4 •

Someday In a parallel universe,
Or maybe a thousand afterlives later.
We would exist;
Me and You.
Where we'll be understood;
Not by the world, but ourselves.
We'd still fights, but this time,
We'd not give up .
The dreams that lives in my mind,
Every night;
Would not be A dream anymore.
And reality, even if unbelievable,
Would be ours to behold.

5. The Storm in My Mind

Overthinking dispatches;
The butterflies;
That lies inside me.
It seizes the emerging,
Blooming flowers;
Inside.
These deliberate thought;
Are the storms in my head;
Ruin the garden;
That my soul holds.

6. Whispers of healing

Piece by piece,I mend the cracks,
Gather light where shadows lack.
The wounds once deep, the scars once sore,
Whisper now- they ache no more.
I'm not broke, just unmade,
A work of love, a soul remade.
Through tinder hands and quiet grace,
I heal, I rise, I find my peace.

7. Silent cries, hidden lies

Unseen feels her,
Sometimes need somebody to see her.
Yet, they told her to smile,
Doesn't matter if it's fake.
Told her to hide her pain;
Put on a happy face;
Well she did what they said;
And she hid it well;
Until the day came,
When her smile fell.

8. Lighting Through Cracks

The heart may break,
yet still it beats,
Through quiet storms,
it finds its peace.
From every crack,
the light will stream,
Healing softly,
like a dream.

9. Invisible in the crowds

I walk through halls that never ends,
faces pass, but none are friends.
Crowded halls, yet I'm unseen
a silent soul caught in between.
Smiles pass, but never stay,
like fleeting sunlight lost in gray.
Coffee shops and campus lights,
groups that form, then fade from sight.
I smile, I nod, I play my part,
but no one hears my quiet heart.

10. The War Within

In the world of
Bright sunshine,
Still struggling with thoughts,
Shivering hands.
Possessing cold smiles,
Empty eyes.
Trapped in a tragedy
Of a mature mind;
And romantic heart
Wrestling to find
Heartsease.

11. Turning The Page

Here's to the end of this chapter;
To all sleepless and
Anxious nights
Ever had.
Releasing all the relationships,
What wasn't our to keep.
And, letting the broken pieces,
To heal again.
As, I smiled,
Since, it was the time
To let go,
And move on..

12. Heart V/S mind

I didn't thought it was surreal,
The fight between;
My heart and mind,
Puzzled me around.
Turned my springing day,
Into a chaos.
Yet this war;
Always leave me,
Breathing rapidly,
Alone !

13. Between Nightmares

I don't wanna be awake right now
But i don't want to go to sleep
Cause I'm scared of my dreams
But is life is just another
So in the end
I've to pick up one night mare
Over the other.

14. The light beyond

Settling beside my old fears,
In the hope
To see the bright light
In the dreary night.
Letting myself drown
Into the ocean eyes.

15. The Path Unknown

Life's a maze of highs and lows,
Chasing dreams where no one knows.
Smiles hide worries, laughs mask pain,
Sunshine comes, then pours the rain.
Trying to find where I belong,
Hoping someday I'll be strong.

16. The present moment

Breathe it in, let time be still,
feel the earth, the air, the thrill.
No past to chase, no future wide,
Just the moment - deep inside.

17. Holding onn...

The clock keeps ticking, never slow,
A thousand thoughts, nowhere to go.
Expectations weigh me down,
Smiles hide the urge to drown.
Breathe in deep, push through the fight,
Hoping one day it feels right

18. Uncertain Paths

The road bends where I cannot see,
A whispered fate calls out to me.
Steps unsteady, doubt runs deep,
Dreams to chase, yet fears to keep.
Between the dusk and breaking day,
I walk the mist, I find my way.

19. Invisible Struggles

Barefoot steps on dusty ground,
Empty hands, yet hope is found.
Smiles persist through days so tough,
Life is cruel, but they stay tough.
I wish the world could truly see,
Their strength, their pain, their dignity.

20. Silent Cries

Another name, another light,
Gone too soon into the night.
Smiles hid the pain inside,
No one saw the tears they cried.
It scares me how the pain runs deep,
I pray for those we couldn't keep.

21. Hello, Goodbye!

A newborn's cry, a breath so new,
A final sigh, a life withdrawn too.
Joy and sorrow, side by side,
One begins, one says goodbye.
In one room hope, in one room pain,
The cycle turns, again, again.

22. Enough!

Her screams are lost in the midnight air,
A world that sees but doesn't care.
Fear walks with her, step by step,
Justice promised, but tears still wept.
How many more before we see?
She deserved to live, to just be free.

23. Live the Moment

The sun sets, the sky glows wide,
Waves rush in, then kiss the tide.
Laughter floats, the world feels light,
Stars wake up to paint the night.
No past, no future—just right now,
Breathe it in, don't ask how.

24. Lost Innocence

I miss the days so free, so bright,
No heavy weight, no sleepless nights.
Barefoot runs and careless dreams,
Now life's a race, or so it seems.
Growing up felt far away,
But now I long for yesterday.

25. Marine Drive Nights

The waves sings softly, calm and free,
The breeze feels like its' hugging me.
City lights shimmer, far yet near,
Lost in the night, free from fear.
For a moment, all feels right,
Lost in the peace, beneath moonlight.

26. Unmeant Pain

I never wished to see them break,
But love's not mine to force or fake.
Their eyes held dreams I couldn't share,
A gentle heart, beyond compare.
I walk away, but still, I know,
I left you standing in my shadow.

27. Dreams to Reality

I wished, I worked, I dared to try,
Now dreams take flight across the sky.
The stars once distant, now shine near,
The path once blurred is bright and clear.
What once was hope is now my view,
A life I dreamed is coming true.

28. Silent Sacrifices

Small hands hold dreams tucked away,
Grown-up burdens too soon to stay.
Smiles are worn to hide the pain,
Silent tears lost in the rain.
A childhood traded, piece by piece,
For love, for hope, for others' peace.

29. Escape

I crave the wind, the open skies,
A place where quiet never dies.
No deadlines, noise, or endless race,
Just me, the world, a slower pace.
To leave it all, just drift away,
And find myself along the way.

30. Never Enough

They chase and grab, yet crave for more,
Drowning rich, but feeling poor.
Gold and silver fill their hands,
Yet empty hearts make no demands.
No matter how much they possess,
Greed leaves them lost in emptiness.

31. Street of Innocence

Tiny hands reach, but none hold tight,
Lost in days that steal their light.
No warm meals, no soft embrace,
Just hollow dreams and weary face.
The world moves on, their cries ignored,
While hunger knocks on broken doors.

32. Unseen

I give my all, yet it's not enough,
Smiles fade, the road stays rough.
Words unspoken, efforts lost,
Love feels distant, cold as frost.
No matter how hard I try to be,
I'm just a shadow—none can see.

33. Shattered Fire

Fury spills like shattered glass,
Words cut deep but never pass.
Drowning in a sea of fire,
Every pulse beats with desire.
Torn between the rage and pain,
Trapped inside this endless chain.

34. Lost in giving

I mend their hearts while mine stays torn,
A silent weight I've always borne.
Their voices loud, my own is small,
I give my all, yet loose it all.
No time to heal, no space to cry,
Just fading fast while days pass by.

35. Love, lost in time

Love now fades like a passing trend,
Lies and games, no hearts to mend.
Loyalty lost, replaced with ease,
Feelings traded like a fleeting breeze.
What once was deep is now so vain,
Love now is pleasure, not the pain.

36. Home, is my heart

• 36 •

Miles away, yet hearts so near,
Home's warm love I long to hear.
City bright, but cold and wide,
I miss my family's side.
Silent nights, a tear or two,
Home, my soul belongs to you.

37. The dance called life

Life moves like wind I cannot chase,
One moment calm, the next—a race.
Plans I made fall out of line,
While fate rewrites the grand design.
Smiles fade, then tears arrive,
Yet somehow still, I feel alive.
Unpredictable, this dance called life

38. Silent betrayal

I called for help, but silence grew,
The faces I trusted simply withdrew.
In my darkest night, no hand to find,
Empty words echo inside my mind.
The smiles were masks, the promises vain,
Now only my shadow knows my pain.
In the ruins of hope, I stand - alone, betrayed.

39. Reflective tone

The wheel of life turns slow but sure,
Each act, each word, will long endure.
What's given out will find its way,
Back to your heart another day.
Good or ill, the circle flies,
A dance beneath the endless skies.

40. Where the heart remains

• 40 •

When laughter fades and roads grow thin,
When strangers leave and storms begin,
One gentle hand will still be near,
A voice of comfort you can hear.
Through every loss, through night and day,
Family is the one that stays,
A quiet home when dreams betray.

41. Still, I Rose

I loved you past the edge of pain,
Through silent storms and endless rain.
You broke me, yet I'd still defend,
Each wound you gave, I'd try to mend.
I wore my heart like it was steel,
But love made dumb what time can't heal.
Now I rise—not whole, but real.

42. The Weight Within

A tightness in the chest,
A weight that won't release,
A discomfort I can't name,
A quiet, burning flame,
That whispers all my fear.
A weight upon my soul,
That pulls me down each day,
Which never fades away.
A fight I can't begin,
To free myself in peace.

43. Weight of Quiet

I thought growing up meant standing tall,
Braving storms with no one to call.
But silence echoed far too loud,
No laughter left within the crowd.
Now I see—it's not the fight,
But hands you hold that make things right.
In overthinking, I missed the light.

44. The Quiet Chaos

It creeps in quiet, steals my breath,
A thousand thoughts that spell out death.
A trembling mind, a racing heart,
No fire outside, yet torn apart.
I smile while storms rage deep inside,
A war I fight, and try to hide.
Anxiety—my silent tide.

45. The Quiet Aftermath

A shattered heart, a silent cry,
Words unspoken, tears run dry.
Promises fade like winter's chill,
Love once bright, now stands still.
Echoes linger, soft and deep,
In the ruins, I learn to weep.

46. The Light of Joy

Happiness blooms like a morning sun,
A gentle breeze, a race well-run.
It sparkles in laughter, soft and bright,
A fleeting moment that feels just right.
In simple joys, it softly stays,
A light that warms our hearts always.

47. Beyond The Horizon

A suitcase packed with dreams so wide,
A heart unsure, but full of pride.
The home behind, the road ahead,
New paths to walk, new words to be said.
The comfort of the past, now far away,
Yet hope will guide with each new day.

48. Content in You

No need to reach for a distant star,
The light you seek is where you are.
In every flaw, a story shines,
In every scar, a mark divine.
Be kind to yourself, let worries flee,
Happiness lives where you let it be.

49. Broken in the Quiet

I held your love like fragile light,
A constant flame through endless night.
You loved me too - I know it's true,
But life wrote paths that splits us in two.
Now silence speaks where words once stayed,
And dreams are debts we have never paid.
Still, my heart aches where yours once lay.

50. To the stars, With Thanks!

I thank the universe, so vast and wide,
For every gift it did provide.
The quiet moments, the lessons learned,
For every bridge and every turn.
In gratitude, my heart does swell,
For all it gave, I am made well.

51. The Last Slice !

• 51 •

One slice left, the room goes still,
My eyes lock on that cheesy thrill.
I move with stealth, a ninja's grace—
But someone else has won the race.
She takes a bite, I drop my knife...
That last slice—that was my life.

The Final Word

As these poems come to a close, may you find a moment of stillness to reflect on the emotions they have stirred. Each word, each line, is a piece of a larger story—one that continues with every person who reads them, feels them, and carries them within. These poems are not just endings, but invitations to keep exploring the quiet spaces of our hearts, to embrace both the light and dark, and to continue healing.

Thank you for joining me on this journey through thought, feeling, and imagination. May these words stay with you long after you turn the final page, offering comfort, understanding, and a sense of connection in a world that often feels fragmented.

Let these words remind you that you are not alone, and that every end is simply a new beginning.

www.ingramcontent.com/pod-product-compliance
Lightning Source LLC
Chambersburg PA
CBHW031803150726
47989CB00006B/2866